DIGGING UP THE PAST

# BIBLICAL SITES

JULIAN BOWSHER

WAYLAND

## DIGGING UP THE PAST

Biblical Sites • Bodies from the Past • Pompeii and Herculaneum • The Search for Dinosaurs • Troy and Knossos • The Valley of the Kings

**Cover background:** The mountain-top palace of Masada. Find out about the story connected to this famous site on page 41.
**Cover inset:** The head of an Ammonite deity (god) dated c.7000 BC from Rabbath-Ammon (modern-day Amman, Jordan).
**Title page:** This is a model of Herod's Temple in Jerusalem, which may be the one Jesus would have known (see pages 38–9).
**Contents page:** This Phoenician ivory was carved in the same period as the ivory decorations for King Ahab's palace at Samaria (see page 33).


**Series and book editor**: Geraldine Purcell
**Series designer**: Joyce Chester
**Book designers:** Malcolm Walker and Helen White
**Consultant**: Jonathan Tubb, Curator of Syria-Palestine in the Western Asiatic Antiquities, British Museum, London





First published in 1996 by Wayland (Publishers) Ltd
61 Western Road, Hove
East Sussex BN3 1JD, England

**British Library Cataloguing in Publication Data**
Bowsher, Julian
Biblical Sites.
(Digging up the Past)
I. Title II. Bull, Peter III. Series
933

ISBN 0 7502 1577 1

DTP design by: Kudos Design and White Design
Printed and bound by L.E.G.O. S.p.A, Vicenza, Italy


**Note:** For the purposes of this book, 'Palestine' refers to the historical region as shown on the map on page 6.

The history of the area of ancient Palestine mentioned in this book spans more than 10,000 years and covers many historical periods.
The chart on page 7 and the timeline on pages 44–5 should help you to place each site or event in time.




**Picture acknowledgements**
The publishers would like to thank the following for allowing their photographs to be reproduced in this book: AKG, London Ltd. 38 (top) (E. Lessing); Peter Clayton 18–19; E. T. Archive 32 (Louvre, Paris); Werner Forman Archive iii and 33 (top) (Iraq Museum, Baghdad/Werner Forman Archive); Michael Holford 9 (British Museum), 12 (top), 16, 20 (both) (bottom/ British Museum), 33 (bottom) (British Museum); Institute of Archaeology, University College London 4–5 (all) (K. Tubb); Courtesy of the Palestine Exploration Fund Photographic Archives, London 12–13, 13 (top), 28 (both), 30 (top), 36 (top); Zev Radovan all other photographs, including cover inset; Cath Senker 43; Tell es-Sa'iyideh Excavation Project 11 (both) (A. Hills); Jonathan Tubb/British Museum 14; ZEFA cover background, 36 (bottom), 40–41, 42 (both).
All artwork is by Peter Bull Art Studio.

# Contents

# Before the Bible

Some of the greatest archaeological discoveries are made by accident. In the early 1980s, when a new highway was being built through the eastern outskirts of Amman, the capital of Jordan, the road engineers did not realize that they had uncovered and nearly destroyed an amazing find. The archaeologists who later went to see what the bulldozers had revealed realized that here was the largest village from the Neolithic (New Stone Age) period (8300–4500 BC) that had ever been found in the whole of the region known as the Near East.

The site was known as 'Ain Ghazal and proper excavations started in 1982, led by an American archaeologist, Dr Gary Rollefson. Only a very small area of the site was investigated but after a few months' work Dr Rollefson's team had learnt much about the remarkable people who had lived there more than eight thousand years earlier.

**◄ One of the 'Ain Ghazal statuettes after being restored.**

**This photograph shows the jumbled remains of the statuettes. ►**

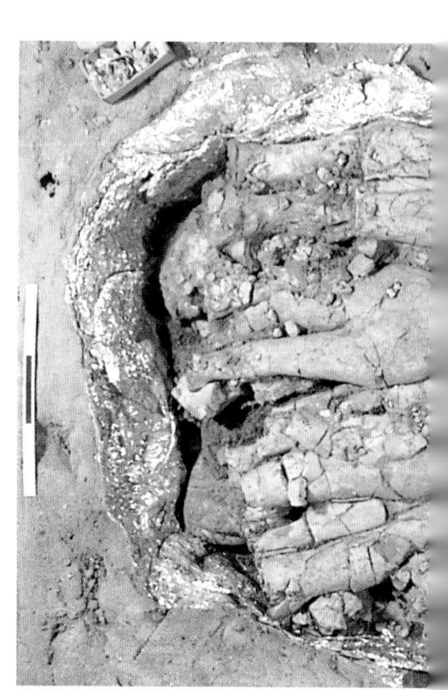

## Early statuettes

▲ **The archaeologists carefully dug round the block of statuettes and prepared it for transport to England.**

In 1983 archaeologists were digging in an area of the site where there were house walls. As they dug down to one of the floor levels they noticed that a large pit had been dug through it. As the earth was scraped away fragments of shaped plaster were seen. After a while the archaeologists were amazed to see the faces of statuettes staring up at them.

Damage from the bulldozers which had been driving less than a metre over the top of the fragile statuettes had left them in a poor condition. It was impossible to excavate them properly where they were, so it was decided to dig around the pit and remove the statuettes all together, in a block. A specialist, Kathryn Tubb, was called in to supervise the removal of the block to her laboratory in England. After months of painstaking work each fragment was individually excavated from the block, which left a large 'jigsaw puzzle' to be put together again. Once this had been done, there were about twenty-five complete statuettes and busts. The figures are not only the earliest human-like statues from the area, they were also probably religious in nature and are amongst the earliest objects of worship from the land of the Bible.

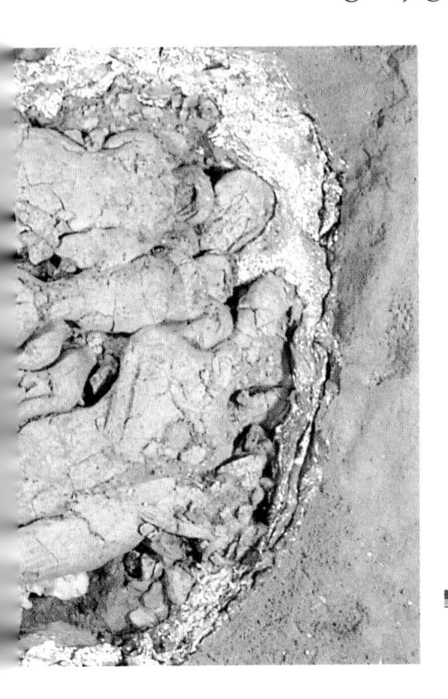

# Early peoples of the Bible lands

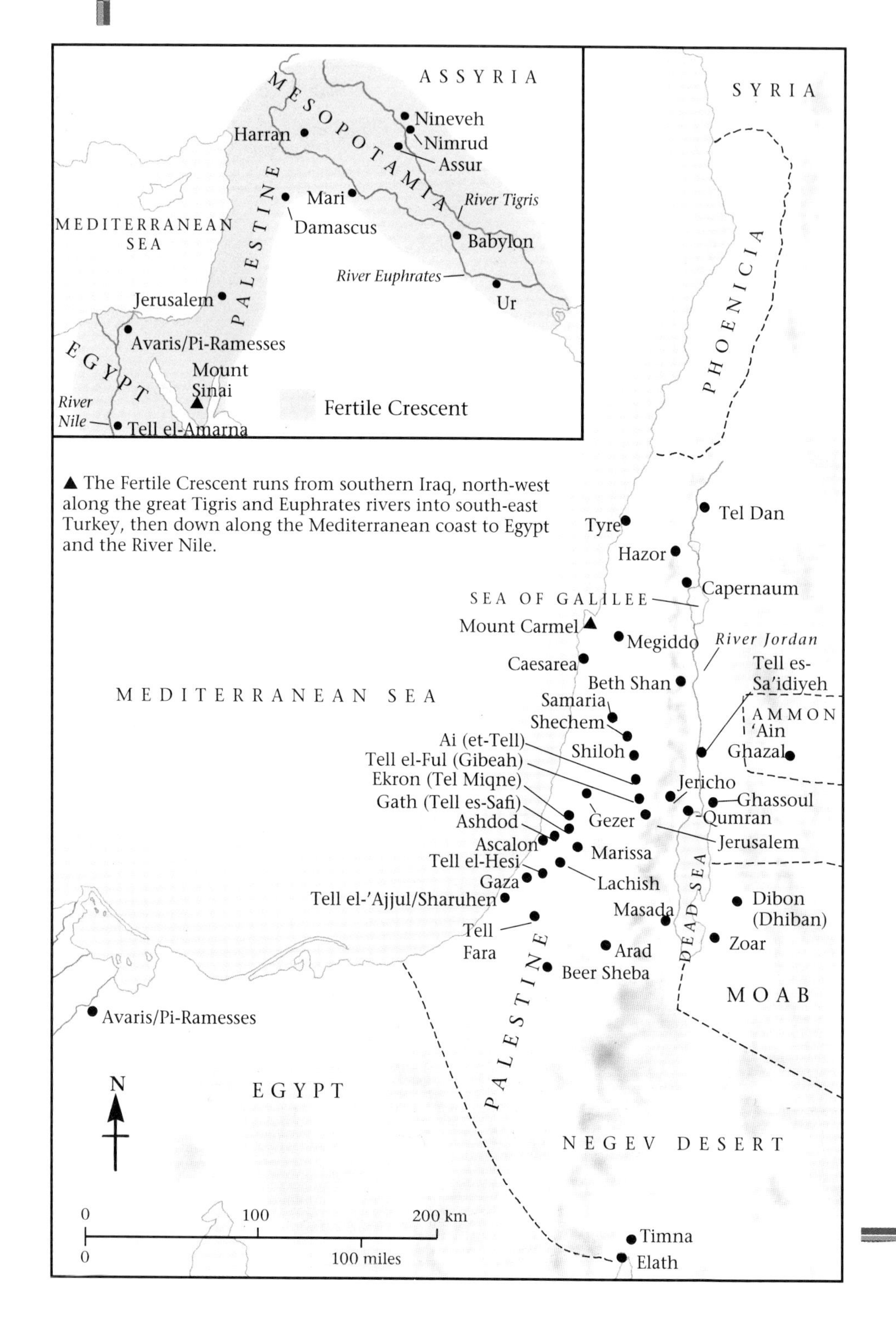


▲ The Fertile Crescent runs from southern Iraq, north-west along the great Tigris and Euphrates rivers into south-east Turkey, then down along the Mediterranean coast to Egypt and the River Nile.

## The land of the Bible

The land of the Bible, known as ancient Palestine, lies at the western end of a great arc known as the Fertile Crescent. The land was very fertile so the farmers of ancient times were able to produce more food than they needed and could trade the surplus. Trade provided the wealth that led to the birth of some of the greatest civilizations of the world. The earliest civilizations developed in Mesopotamia, a region which lay between two great rivers – the Tigris and the Euphrates. To the north was the kingdom of Syria and to the south, the powerful Egyptian empire. The Bible stories show that people traded throughout this large area.

## The early peoples

Much of the history of the early civilizations in the Bible lands was learnt through excavations led by the British archaeologist Dame Kathleen Kenyon at Jericho between 1952 and 1958. There were many large villages, like 'Ain Ghazal (see pages 4–5), but Jericho was one of the first walled towns. In about 7000 BC the settlement was surrounded by great stone walls with ten-metre high towers along them. The people of Jericho also made statuettes and plastered the skulls of their ancestors with clay. By about 6000 BC the Neolithic peoples had also learnt to make pottery.

**▲ This body of a man, from a cave near Mount Carmel, dates from about 10000 BC. He was buried wearing a beaded head-dress.**

**▲ A stone tower from the Neolithic period at Jericho.**

### Chronology of the Bible lands

|  |  |
| --- | --- |
| Neolithic (New Stone Age) | 8300–4500 BC |
| Chalcolithic | 4500–3200 BC |
| Early Bronze Age | 3200–2000 BC |
| Middle Bronze Age | 2000–1550 BC |
| Late Bronze Age | 1550–1150 BC |
| Iron Age | 1200–612 BC |
| Babylonian and Persian periods | 612–332 BC |
| Hellenistic Period | 332–63 BC |
| Roman Period | 63 BC–AD 324 |
| Byzantine Period | AD 324–640 |
| Early Arab Period | AD 640–1099 |

## Chalcolithic sites

From 4300 BC the number of settlements in Palestine had increased greatly. Due to the improvements made in farming and, above all, in metalworking, this period was called the Chalcolithic period (4500–3200 BC), from the Greek word for copper, *khalkos*. At Timna, in the Negev Desert, there were copper mines and makeshift houses where the miners lived, complete with household shrines. The skill of the coppersmiths of this period was revealed by the discovery, in 1961, of a hoard of 436 beautiful copper objects. They were found in Nahal Mishmar, a cave settlement in the mountains west of the Dead Sea, by an Israeli archaeologist, Pessah Bar-Adon.

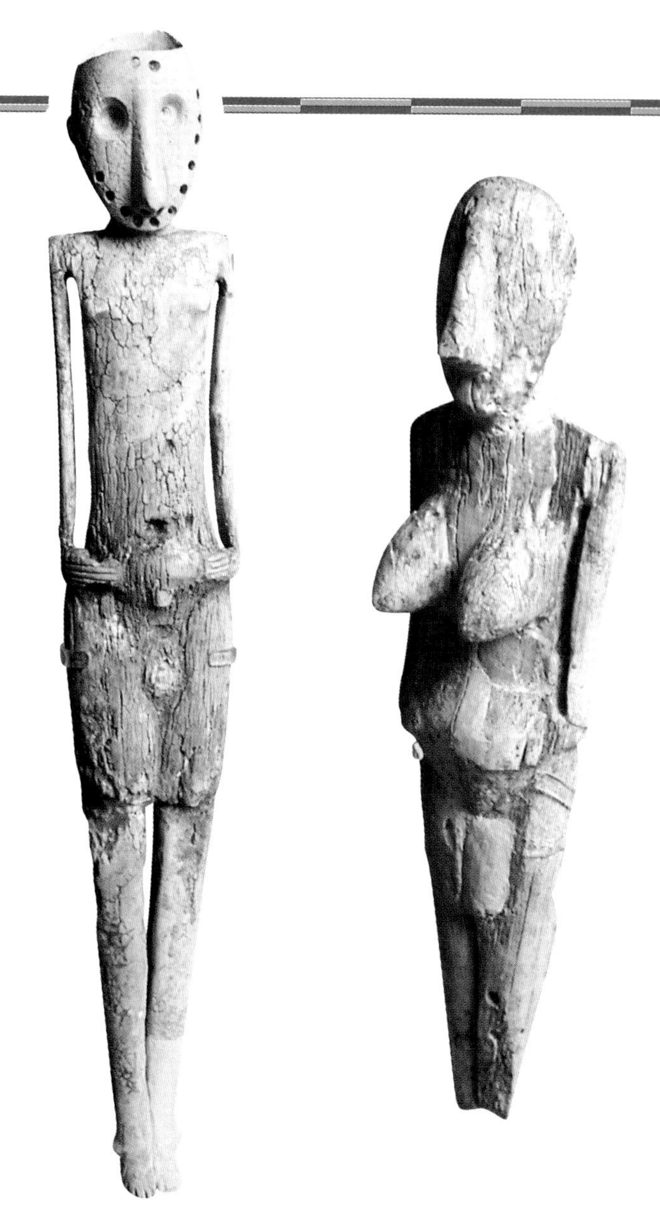

**▲ The peoples of the Chalcolithic period were great artists. These figures, from Beer Sheba, are carved from ivory.**

One of the most famous Chalcolithic sites has been uncovered at Ghassoul in the Jordan Valley by three separate excavations since 1929. These excavations uncovered a large village of rectangular mud-brick houses. Many of the houses had their walls painted with figures and geometric designs, like the one shown here.

# Archaeology and the Bible

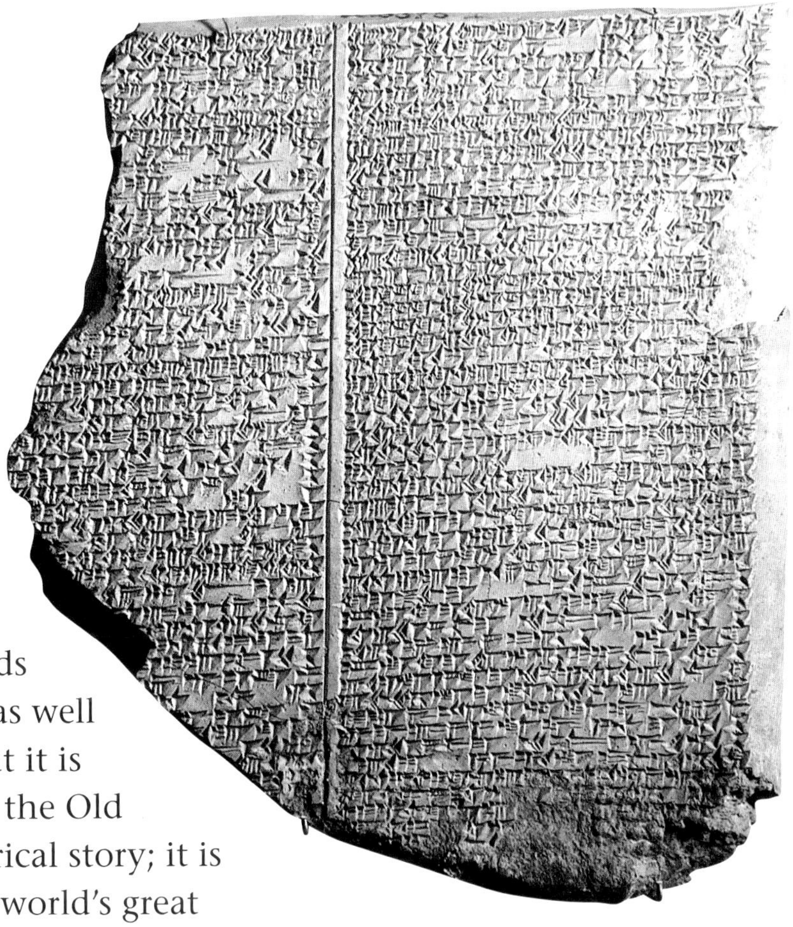

The Old Testament of the Bible is a collection of religious writings concerning the special relationship that the Jewish people, the 'Children of Israel', believe they have with God. It records the history of these peoples as well as their laws and religion. But it is important to remember that the Old Testament is not just a historical story; it is the sacred text of two of the world's great religions, Judaism and Christianity. Much of this history is seen by many as sacred history. The holy book of Islam, the Qur'an, is regarded by Muslims as the completion of the Biblical account.

Not everything written in the Bible can possibly be confirmed by archaeological discoveries but the accounts of events often cannot be proved wrong either. There is simply no other evidence for many of the events described in the Bible and they remain a matter of faith.

**▲ The story of the world being covered by a flood is not just found in the Bible. This Babylonian tablet, which tells the story of a great flood in Mesopotamia, may be older than the Biblical account.**

▲ **The earliest versions of the Old Testament and Qur'an were written on long sheets of papyrus and rolled up into scrolls like this.**

The Old Testament was probably only written down from about 700 BC onwards. Many of the stories were based on tales passed down through generations and it is difficult to provide an exact date for the earlier stories.

## The Bible as reference

The Bible remains an important document for any study of the archaeology of ancient Palestine. Until about 150 years ago the Bible was the only known historical reference for the area but since then thousands of ancient inscriptions and texts have been discovered in the regions of the neighbouring ancient civilizations of Egypt, Mesopotamia and Syria.

Archaeological excavations in and around ancient Palestine have sometimes provided evidence for the existence of places, peoples and events recorded in the Bible. But these excavations have also revealed other historical information not mentioned in the Bible.

The New Testament of the Bible is the collection of religious writings concerning the life and teachings of Jesus. There are many other accounts from Greek and Roman writers covering this period. Archaeologists can use these writings to help them confirm the Bible stories.

## Tells

The landscape of the Bible lands includes hundreds of ancient sites. The most obvious sites are the great mounds known as 'tells' which represent the layers built up over centuries of cities built on top of each other. Many of these tells have been occupied for periods of between one and two thousand years and sometimes include up to twenty layers of debris and remains of buildings, each one representing a different period of time. The oldest buildings, such as those at 'Ain Ghazal and Jericho, were built of stone. From the Early Bronze Age (3200–2000 BC) most were made out of mud brick, making it difficult for archaeologists to distinguish between the buildings and the earth around them.

**An archaeologist examining the different layers of a tell. ▼**

**◄ One of the large tells that dominate the landscape of the Bible lands. This one is at Tell es-Sa'idiyeh where recent excavations have shown that it dates back at least to the Early Bronze Age.**

▲ The outside of the Church of the Holy Sepulchre, in Jerusalem, showing different styles of architecture that have been added over the years.

## Early archaeology

Since the Byzantine period (AD 324–640) many pilgrims have travelled to the 'Holy Land' in search of Christian remains. Some of the earliest excavations are believed to have been made by Empress Helena, mother of the Byzantine emperor Constantine the Great (AD 280–337). She found, in a cave in Jerusalem, what she believed to be the cross on which Jesus Christ was crucified. To mark and protect the spot Constantine built the Church of the Holy Sepulchre, which still stands today.

In the 1830s the American archaeologist Edward Robinson set off on a journey of exploration during which he identified many sites mentioned in the Bible. It must be said that many of the early archaeologists were keen to prove that the Bible was a true record of events in history.

## PEF survey

In 1865 the Palestine Exploration Fund (PEF) was founded in London for the scientific study of the Bible lands. In 1867, Captain Charles Warren was sent to Jerusalem where he dug deep shafts to try and find the age of the city walls. His methods were crude and dangerous by today's standards but they provided a basis for modern study. The greatest achievement of the PEF in the last century was the *Survey of Western Palestine* which for the first time

When Frederick Bliss excavated at Tell el-Hesi he used trucks on tramlines to take debris away. ▶

provided accurate maps of the country marked with the ruins of many sites. These were often identified with the ancient sites mentioned in the Bible.

## Flinders Petrie and Tell el-Hesi

The first proper scientific excavation in Palestine was carried out in 1890, when the British archaeologist William Flinders Petrie dug the site of Tell el-Hesi. Petrie had been working in Egypt where he had become one of the greatest archaeologists of the day. At Tell el-Hesi he systematically excavated each of the layers, dating them by the pottery and other objects he found in them. Petrie went back to Egypt the following year but work at Tell el-Hesi was continued by the American archaeologist, Frederick Bliss. In 1899 Bliss was joined by a young Irishman, Robert Macalister, in excavating four tells in southern Palestine, including Marissa (see page 36). In 1902 Macalister started excavations at the Biblical city of Gezer, in central Palestine, and published a detailed account of his findings.

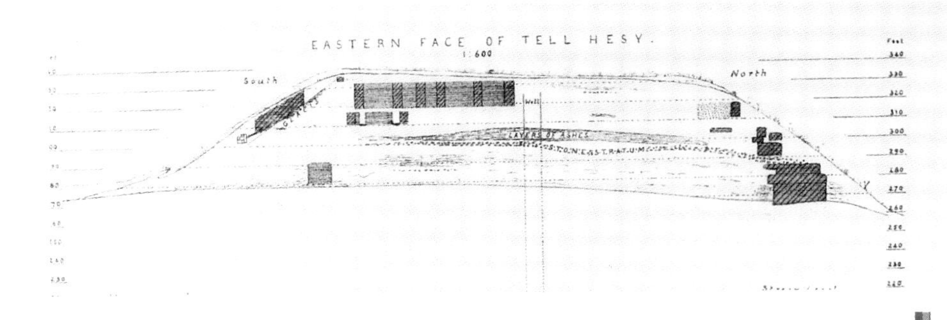


▲ **A drawing by Flinders Petrie of his excavations at Tell el-Hesi, which showed how he understood the build-up of the different layers within the tell.**

The American archaeologist William Albright excavated Tell Beit Mirsim, between 1926 and 1932. Here he carried out studies in dating pottery used from 3000 BC to the end of the Iron Age period (1200–612 BC).

# The Patriarchs and the first cities

## The coming of the Canaanites

It seems that new peoples came into the Bible lands in about 3200 BC. Excavations during the 1960s by Joseph Callaway at the site of Ai, north of Jerusalem, showed that the earliest levels contained a mixture of late Chalcolithic pottery and new material not seen in the area before. This time marks the beginning of the Early Bronze Age and these newcomers to the region are known to us as the Canaanites. Their civilization is an important feature of the Bible accounts.

### The Patriarchs

The Patriarchs of the Old Testament, Abraham, Isaac, Jacob and Joseph, are historical characters from a period shrouded in legend and it is difficult to work out exactly when they may have lived. Nevertheless most archaeologists think that this period lasted much longer than the four generations stated in the *Book of Genesis* – the first book, or chapter, of the Bible. They believe it covered much of what we call the Early Bronze Age.

**◄ Typical Canaanite clay pots from the Early Bronze Age, excavated from Tell es-Sa'idiyeh.**

▲ An aerial view of the Canaanite city of Arad.

▲ (inset) A detail of the restored walls of Canaanite Arad, showing a tower wall.

## Canaanite cities

The Early Bronze Age is the period when proper city life began in Palestine and the great tells were founded. Most of them were built at important locations, in fertile land and on trade routes. The Early Bronze Age was a period of busy trade and great wealth. At Tell es-Sa'idiyeh, east of the River Jordan, an olive oil 'factory' dating from this period was found by British archaeologist Jonathan Tubb, which revealed an organized use of the land. The Canaanites introduced new architecture and city layouts. The 'new' Canaanite city at Ai was surrounded by high walls and contained an impressive temple with columns supporting the roof. Similar cities were founded at Beth Shan, Hazor, Jericho, Lachish, Megiddo and Arad. At Arad, in southeast Palestine, the city walls had great semicircular towers of the type seen in a wall-painting from the same period at a tomb at Deshasheh in Egypt. Excavations at Arad by the Israeli archaeologist Ruth Amiran revealed a whole town plan with streets, private houses, temples and administrative buildings.

▲ **Ur was the capital of the Sumerian civilization in 3000 BC. This decorated box, known as the Standard of Ur, shows the great artistry of the Sumerians.**

## Abraham – the route from the city of Ur

Abraham, one of the Patriarchs, is regarded as the ancestor of both Jews and Arabs. The Bible tells us that his family originally came from the great city of Ur, in southern Mesopotamia, present-day Iraq. Between 1922 and 1934, extensive excavations by a British archaeologist, Sir Leonard Woolley, revealed that the city had a history stretching back to at least 3000 BC.

From Ur, Abraham and his family would have travelled north along the River Euphrates and may have stopped at Mari, a major trading city. The Bible records that Abraham and his family spent some years in Harran, in southern Turkey, and from there finally travelled down into Canaan and settled at Shechem. Archaeological excavations have shown that, by the Early Bronze Age, when Abraham is thought to have lived, Shechem can have been no more than a small village.

## The Cities of the Plain

The Cities of the Plain – Sodom, Gomorrah, Admah, Zeboim and Zoar – were well known for their wickedness, according to a story in the *Book of Genesis*. This account tells how God was displeased with the people of these cities and decided to destroy them by fire. The story tells us that God told Lot, Abraham's nephew, to go from the city and not look back at the destruction. Lot fled from Sodom with his wife and children but his wife looked back at the city and was turned into a pillar of salt. Lot and his two daughters stayed in Zoar for a while but were advised to move on and then found shelter in a cave in the mountains.

**▲ A typical landscape at the southern end of the Dead Sea, with a natural pillar often associated with the story of Lot's wife.**

## Lot's wife and the pillars of salt

There are a number of naturally formed salt pillars in the area around the Dead Sea, which may have been the basis for the story of the fate of Lot's wife. Archaeologists have searched for years for evidence of the Cities of the Plain, which were supposedly destroyed. Since the Byzantine period Zoar had been identified as the town of Safi. In the 1970s a detailed archaeological survey did find five major sites (including Safi) that dated to the Early Bronze Age. Also excavations have revealed that they were large settlements and that several had indeed been destroyed by fire. The Cities of the Plain were shown to have been destroyed by about 2400 BC. We do not know why they were destroyed but it is important to note that many of the other great cities, such as Ai and Jericho, were also deserted at about this time.

# The might of Egypt

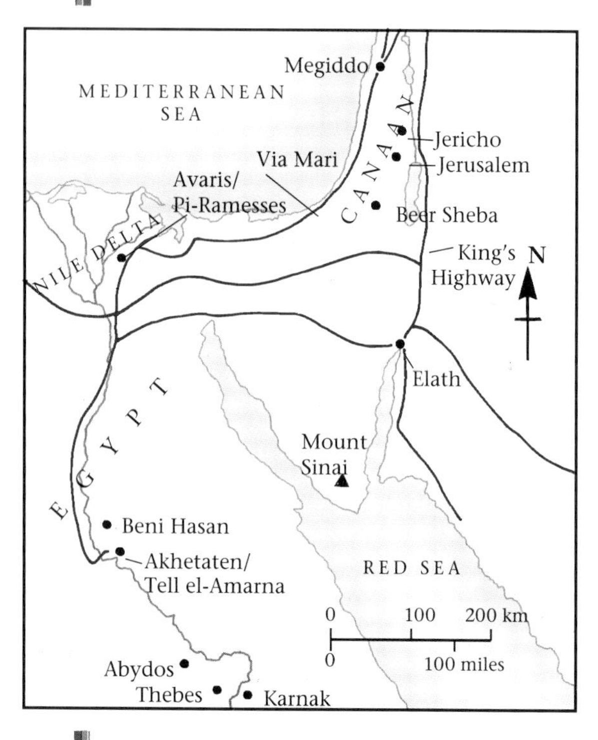


▲ **This map shows important sites in Egypt during the Middle Bronze Age and trade routes to and from Canaan.**

Much of the history of Palestine is bound up with its powerful neighbour, Egypt. Indeed, much of the dating of archaeological sites in Palestine comes from the Egyptians, for they kept records of nearly every aspect of their lives, in paintings and carved reliefs, and in texts inscribed on stone and written on papyrus.

Egypt's connection with Palestine began in the Early Bronze Age and a number of Egyptian objects, mostly luxury goods, have been found on Early Bronze Age sites in Palestine. Canaanite objects have been found in Egypt, especially in the early Egyptian royal tombs at Abydos. The Egyptians were also at war with the cities in Palestine from time to time.

## Middle Bronze Age (2000–1550 BC) – Canaanite traders

The wall-painting from a tomb at Beni Hasan, Egypt, dates from about 1900 BC and clearly shows Canaanite peoples coming into Egypt to trade. So many Canaanites came that when the Egyptian Middle Kingdom collapsed in about 1700 BC these newcomers were able to seize

power throughout Lower Egypt. The new rulers were known as the Hyksos, meaning 'rulers of foreign lands'. Their capital at Avaris in the Nile Delta has been identified as Tell el Dab'a. This site has been excavated by an Austrian archaeologist, Manfred Bietak, since 1966. Bietak has found a lot of Canaanite material, which showed that the Hyksos rulers introduced bronze working, weaving and the wheeled chariot into Egypt.

## Joseph

The story of Joseph almost certainly relates to this period. The Bible tells how he rose to become the chief minister to the pharaoh, or king, (who was probably a Hyksos), and rode in a chariot.

**The wall-painting from Beni Hasan shows two Egyptian officials escorting a group of people, perhaps Canaanites, who are carrying their wares into Egypt to trade. ▼**

In about 1550 BC the native Egyptian rulers, based at Thebes in the south, led a revolt against the Hyksos and eventually defeated them and chased them out of the country. The Hyksos retreated to Palestine, the land of their origin, and the Egyptians followed with a full-scale invasion. Palestine became an Egyptian province during the Late Bronze Age period (1550–1150 BC). In this period Egypt became a great world power and Egyptian armies reached as far as the River Euphrates. In 1468 BC the pharaoh Tuthmosis III defeated a Canaanite army at Megiddo in northern Palestine and eventually brought the area under Egyptian control.

In the fourteenth century BC, during the reign of pharaoh Akhenaten, Egypt's power became weaker. Akhenaten moved the capital from Thebes to a new site called Akhetaten, known today as Tell el-Amarna. Here in 1884 a peasant woman came across a hoard of clay tablets with a form of writing on them. These turned out to be letters addressed to the Egyptian royal court, including some written by the rulers of the Canaanite cities. These writings are now known as the Amarna Letters.

▲ A statue of Ramesses II holding an offering table.

▲ One of the Amarna Letters written by a king in northern Syria to the pharaoh Akhenaten asking for friendship.

## Ramesses II – building projects

Further campaigns by Seti I and his son Ramesses II restored Egyptian power in Palestine, but many of the great cities were reduced in size while others were built up as Egyptian strongholds. It was Ramesses II who was famous for his great building operations, including the temples at Abu Simbel. He also rebuilt the old Hyksos capital, Avaris, and renamed it Pi-Ramesses. An important reference to Egypt in the Bible is retold on pages 26–7.

# The flowering of Canaan

The Canaanite civilization began in the Early Bronze Age; the Canaanites were probably the ancestors of most of the peoples in the land of the Bible. The great cities that they founded rose to importance again in the period known to archaeologists as the Middle Bronze Age, which was a time of great prosperity in Canaan. The establishment of the Egyptian Middle Kingdom brought steady rule and reopened the trade routes. Egyptian texts record many of the great Canaanite cities as flourishing. It was a period when craftspeople and artists made beautiful pottery, metalwork and ivory carvings. There was trading throughout the Near East, and luxury goods brought in from Greece, Cyprus, Syria, Turkey and Egypt are also found on many sites.



▲ This map shows some important sites in the region of Canaan.

A Middle Bronze Age jar found at Jericho, made in the form of a human head. ►

◄ **Some of the gold jewellery, pendants and belt fittings, found by Flinders Petrie at Tell el-‘Ajjul.**

## Treasure from Tell el-‘Ajjul

In 1932 Flinders Petrie returned to Palestine to excavate a large mound known as Tell el-‘Ajjul. The size and riches of this site have led modern archaeologists to identify it with the Hyksos city of Sharuhen. Petrie himself believed that ‘Ajjul was ancient Gaza and that the city of Sharuhen was at the smaller Tell Fara which he had excavated a few years earlier. Egyptian objects such as scarab seals and even small statuettes were found at both sites. Beneath the floor of a great palace at ‘Ajjul was found a hoard of beautiful gold jewellery including necklaces, pendants and earrings. More gold jewellery was found in the tombs next to the city, which were excavated in 1930–34.

## Hazor temples and an altar at Gezer

Hazor in northern Palestine was probably the largest and most powerful city of the Middle Bronze Age. Excavations in the 1960s by an Israeli archaeologist, Yigael Yadin, revealed a series of great temples surrounded by walls in the northern quarter of the city of Hazor, one of which contained statues and an altar. Robert Macalister had found an open-air ‘high place’, typical of those described in the Bible, at Gezer in 1902–9.

## Great buildings

During Egyptian occupation, at the beginning of the Late Bronze Age, Palestine entered an era of peace and stability, with renewed trade connections. New, impressive buildings were erected in Canaanite cities. At Megiddo, an earlier gateway built of mud brick was replaced by a stone one in the Late Bronze Age. Excavations in the 1960s by Yadin revealed a great palace near the gateway which contained beautiful carved ivories and jewellery. At Shechem a three-chambered temple was found within the walled city. The city of Dan is mentioned amongst the conquests of the pharaoh Tuthmosis III and it was still a great city when it was mentioned in the Amarna Letters.

**▲ An aerial view of the tell of Megiddo shows the surrounding walls which were used as fortifications.**

However, under Ramesses II the Egyptians strengthened a number of cities whilst letting some of the others fall into decline. Hazor was still mentioned in the Amarna Letters as a great city, even controlling other smaller ones, but it later declined.

### Defensive action

Excavations of great Canaanite cities have shown an important development in fortifications from the Middle Bronze Age period. The building up of a tell, layer by layer over the centuries, provided some defence because an attacking army would have the difficult task of fighting while moving up a slope. Extra defences, such as surrounding the city with a great wall, were also successful. Another form of defence was to use the slopes of the tell as a barrier to attackers by thickening and covering it with a coating of plaster – which made it slippery. This is known as a *glacis* and remains of these slopes have been found at many sites including Hazor, Jericho, ‘Ajjul, Gezer and Lachish.

## Beth Shan – Egyptian remains

One city that the Egyptians chose as a regional capital was Beth Shan and excavations here have unearthed more Egyptian material than at any other site in Palestine. During the Late Bronze Age the Egyptians built palaces for their governors and these have been found at Beth Shan and on the east bank of the River Jordan at Tell es-Sa'idiyeh (ancient Zarethan). Garrisons of Egyptian troops were also stationed at these sites.

**▲ A typical Philistine coffin found at Beth Shan. Philistine troops guarded Egyptian strongholds in ancient Palestine sometime after 1200 BC.**

## The Sea Peoples – the Philistines arrive

An important development in the last centuries of the Late Bronze Age was the emergence of a group of raiders known by the Egyptians as the Sea Peoples. It is not known exactly where they came from, perhaps the Aegean region or southern Turkey, but they started attacking the coasts of Syria, Palestine and Egypt from about 1200 BC. They appear to have been made up of many tribes, of which the most famous were the Philistines. After the Egyptians defeated the Sea Peoples they then employed the Philistines as garrison troops at strongholds in Palestine such as Beth Shan, Tell Fara, Gezer and Lachish. The evidence for this comes from the distinctive coffins used by the Philistines, which have been found at these sites. The Philistines did leave another lasting impact on the country; it was called Palestine after them.

## Great Philistine cities

The Bible refers to five main Philistine cities along the coast: Ascalon, Ashdod, Gaza, Ekron and Gath. Earlier excavations at the first two sites have shown that there were Early Bronze Age settlements at these sites which were destroyed in the thirteenth century BC and then taken over by the new Philistine cities. Ekron and Gath have only recently been identified, at the sites of Tel Miqne (Ekron) and Tell es-Safi (Gath). Excavations have revealed that Ekron was one of the largest of the Philistine cities.

▲ Oil presses excavated in a Philistine house at Tel Miqne (Ekron).

## Egyptians leave – beginning of the Iron Age

Around 1150 BC the Egyptians finally gave up control of Palestine. The settlement of the Philistines there usually marks the end of the Late Bronze Age and the beginning of the Iron Age. Indeed, changes were felt throughout the Near East at this time and by 1100 BC the Canaanite civilization was itself starting to decline in Palestine. But a distinct group of Canaanites continued to thrive on the northern coast where they became known as the Phoenicians.

◄ In 1948 at Tell Qasile, on the outskirts of Tel Aviv, an excavation uncovered a Philistine temple which used pillars of cedar wood. This picture shows one of the small open-air shrines next to the temple.

# The coming of the Israelites

## Captivity in Egypt

The Amarna Letters refer to a rebel group within Palestine as the Hapiru. It is thought that these peoples should be identified with the Hebrews of the Bible. The Hebrews, said to be the descendants of Jacob, were also known as the 'Children of Israel'.

### Moses

The Bible tells of a Hebrew baby being found by an Egyptian princess. When he grew up Moses became an important person in Egypt and a favourite of the pharaoh. When he saw how the Hebrew people were cruelly treated and forced to work on building projects Moses decided to ask the pharaoh to release the Hebrews from their captivity. The pharaoh refused so Moses warned that God would bring plagues to Egypt – the final and worst being the death of every Egyptian first-born child.

After this final disaster the pharaoh allowed Moses to lead the Hebrews out of Egypt. This is called the 'Exodus'. The Egyptian army followed the Hebrews to force them to return but, once they reached the Red Sea, Moses prayed to God to part the waters to allow the Hebrews to cross. Once they were across, the sea crashed in over the Egyptian army which had tried to follow. So, the Hebrew people were free to continue to their homeland of Canaan in ancient Palestine.

The story in the Bible of a period of captivity in Egypt refers to the large numbers of Hapiru, or Hebrews, captured during the campaigns of Seti I. The Bible records that they were put to work building the city of Pi-Ramesses. In a rare confirmation of a Biblical account, Egyptian records state that Hapiru people were indeed employed on the building works of Ramesses II – the son of Seti I.

Hittite texts from the same time also refer to the Hapiru as homeless peoples. Some historians therefore believe that the Hapiru were people who were driven from the main cities by the Egyptians and established themselves in small hill settlements that appeared towards the end of the Late Bronze Age.

## Exodus from Egypt

▲ A remarkable painting from the walls of a synagogue at Dura Europos near the River Euphrates, dating to the mid-third century AD. The scene shows Moses as both central figures. On the right, Moses is closing the Red Sea with Egyptians drowning in it. On the left, Moses is with the 'Children of Israel' marching into the Sinai Desert.

Any 'Exodus' or escape of the 'Children of Israel' from Egypt was probably linked with the upheavals in the region as Egyptian rule over Palestine was coming to an end. The unnamed pharaoh of the Exodus story in the Bible was almost certainly Ramesses II. The hero of the Exodus was Moses, about whom little is known except that he had an Egyptian name! It is also thought that the route taken out of Egypt was through one of the reed seas or marshes at the Nile Delta, rather than through the Red Sea.

## Joshua's triumphs – fact or fiction?

The military conquests mentioned in the books of *Exodus, Joshua* and *Judges* appear to be contradicted by archaeological findings. After wandering in the Sinai Desert, the 'Children of Israel' are said to have travelled up the east side of the Jordan River and destroyed the cities of Bozrah and Heshbon. However, excavations have shown that these two sites did not come into existence until hundreds of years later.

It is written in the Bible that the invasion of Canaan was led by Moses' general and successor Joshua, but this story has also caused problems. Amongst the cities Joshua's army is said to have destroyed was Jericho. The Bible account recalls how the sound of the army's trumpets caused the walls to collapse.

▲ Mrs Garstang supervising local workers at the excavations at Jericho in the early 1930s.

## Did Jericho's walls come tumbling down?

In 1930 John Garstang excavated the site of Jericho and found a collapsed wall round the site, which he believed dated to the time of Joshua. This appeared to confirm the Biblical story. However, more scientific work conducted by Kathleen Kenyon twenty years later revealed that Garstang's walls dated from the Early Bronze Age, a thousand years earlier than Garstang had thought and before Joshua's time. Kenyon also found that, although there had been a Middle Bronze Age city at Jericho, it was not lived in at the time of Joshua.

## Ai – another city not destroyed by Joshua

Excavations in the 1960s at Ai, also said to have been destroyed by Joshua, revealed that after its rich Early Bronze Age history it was destroyed in about 2350 BC and not occupied again until after Joshua's time. The modern Arabic name of this site is et-Tell, which means 'the ruined mound', and the old Biblical Hebrew name, *Ai,* also means 'ruins'. It seems that when the account in the *Book of Joshua* came to be written down, the original name of the city had long been forgotten but its physical remains led the new settlement to be called Ai, or 'Ruins'. Only at the city of Hazor have excavations revealed a destruction layer, of burnt ash, dated to the middle of the thirteenth century BC. This was associated, according to Yigael Yadin, with Joshua, who is said to have burnt down the city.

More excavation work at Jericho during the 1930s. ▼

## Israelites

It is increasingly thought by modern archaeologists and historians that the so-called conquest of Canaan was a very gradual process that involved the Hapiru/Hebrew people within the country as well as those returning from Egypt. Excavations at the small hill settlements throughout Palestine have revealed the growth of a new culture, that we call 'Israelite', beginning in the thirteenth to twelfth centuries BC. This change was, it seems, more of a cultural and spiritual conquest than a military one. From this period Yahweh, or Jehovah, became the only God of the 'Children of Israel'. The first mention outside the Bible of 'Israel' as a nation comes from a victory stele set up by the pharaoh Merneptah in about 1230 BC.

## The Philistines and Saul

It was after this shadowy 'conquest period' that there is definite evidence of early Israelite occupation. The Bible relates that after Joshua's 'conquest' of Canaan he put the Ark of the Covenant (see the box on the right) in the city of Shiloh. Excavations of Shiloh have shown that the site seems to have been a religious centre for much of its history and many centuries later Byzantine churches and Muslim mosques were also built there. A layer of ash from a great fire dating from the eleventh century BC has been linked with the Philistine destruction of the site.

The Bible suggests that the first Israelite king, Saul, led an army against the Philistines. Some people think that Saul may not have been a real person but a folk hero who represented a rallying force against the Philistines.

## The Commandments

According to the Bible, during the long 'Exodus' journey through the desert Moses went up Mount Sinai, where he was told by God to write down the Ten Commandments – the laws and rules God expected people to follow. The Commandments were written on stone tablets. When Moses returned from the mountain he found the people worshipping an idol and behaving badly. In his anger Moses smashed the tablets before the crowd. The pieces were gathered up and placed in a golden container, called the Ark of the Covenant – which became an important symbol of the agreement made by the Hebrews to follow God's laws.

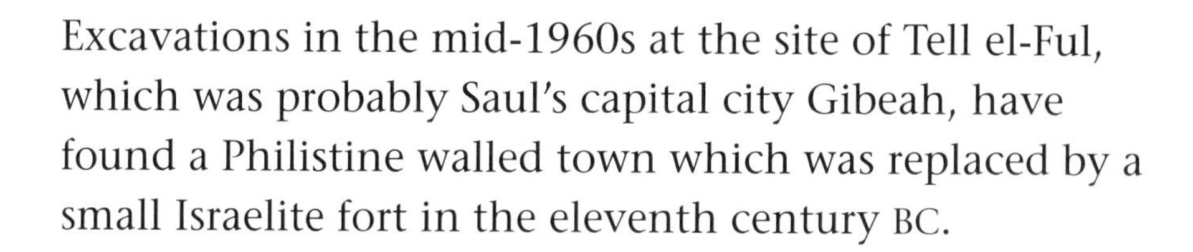

Excavations in the mid-1960s at the site of Tell el-Ful, which was probably Saul's capital city Gibeah, have found a Philistine walled town which was replaced by a small Israelite fort in the eleventh century BC.

**A photograph of Tell el-Ful (Gibeah) taken in 1920.▼**

The war against the Philistines went on for many years. One episode in the Bible tells how Jonathan, the son of Saul, captured a Philistine stronghold called Michmash by finding a secret passage around the back. In modern times, during the First World War (1914–18), advancing British troops found themselves held up by Turks occupying the same hill. The officer in charge read through his Bible, found the same passage and captured the hill in the same way as Jonathan had nearly three thousand years before!

## King David

David was the first great king of the Old Testament – in which many of his deeds are told – but it was only in 1993 that an excavation at the city of Dan, in northern Palestine, found the first mention of David outside the Bible. The archaeologists were drawing plans of a room that dated to the ninth century BC when one of them noticed that one of the building stones had an ancient inscription on it. The stone, which had been reused as a building block, turned out to be part of a stele that celebrated the victory of a Syrian king against, among others, 'the House of David'.

**◄ The stone from Tel Dan, written in Syrian script known as Aramaic, mentioning victories against the 'House of David'.**

## King Solomon – the great builder

David reigned between about 1000 and 960 BC and was followed by his son Solomon. According to the Bible the reign of Solomon was one of great wealth and building activity. Archaeological work has revealed buildings of this time but they were not as grand as the Bible suggests.

## Excavations at Megiddo

The identification of Solomon's fortifications is one of the great detective stories of modern archaeology. It began around 1903 at Gezer, where Robert Macalister found wall towers that he thought were from the period of Solomon and a building that he identified as a fort of the Hellenistic (Greek) period (332–63 BC). At Megiddo at the same time a German team found similar wall towers, and later American excavators found a gateway there. In 1955, when Yigael Yadin was excavating the city of Hazor, he found a great gateway with three rooms on either side that seemed to date from the time of Solomon. He then remembered that the *Book of Kings* said that Solomon *'built the cities of Hazor, Megiddo and Gezer'* and looked up the original excavation records of the earlier digs at Gezer and Megiddo. He saw that the Megiddo gateway was of the same type as that at Hazor and that Macalister's 'Hellenistic fort' at Gezer was really another gateway from King Solomon's time.

**The gateway from Hazor, reconstructed in the Israel Museum, Jerusalem. ▼**

# Kings and conquerors

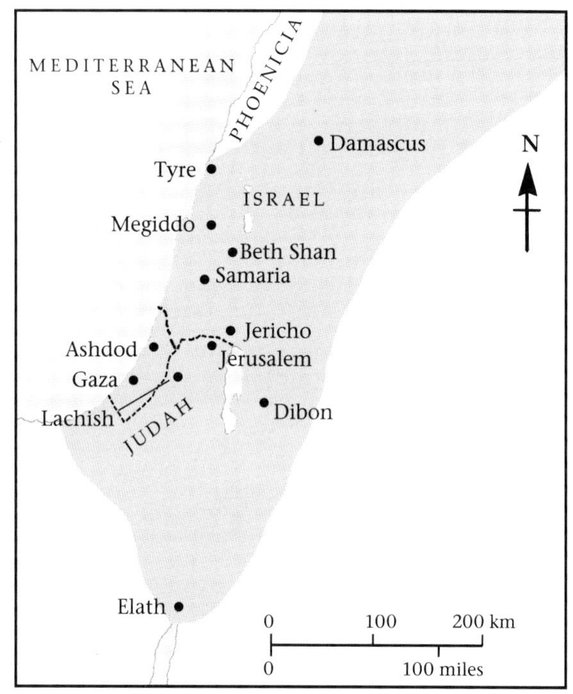


## Palestine split – Judah and Israel

After the death of Solomon in 930 BC the kingdom founded by Saul was split in two, Judah in the south and Israel in the north (see map on left). Almost immediately, however, the Egyptian pharaoh Sheshonq (Shishak in the Bible) invaded both kingdoms. Excavations have revealed traces of his route at Megiddo, where he destroyed a palace of the time of Solomon. Nevertheless, this was generally a peaceable period and archaeology has revealed no great developments in the area.

In Judah, King Rehoboam rebuilt Lachish and made it into one of the most powerful cities in the land. King Omri of Israel founded Samaria as his new capital. Omri had tried to invade the kingdom of Moab across the River Jordan but after the Moabite king, Mesha, fought back he erected a great stele naming his beaten enemies, including Omri. The stele dates to about 830 BC and was found in the village of Dhiban (Biblical Dibon) by a German priest in 1868. He made a copy of the inscription but by the time other archaeologists got there the local people had broken it up in order to sell the pieces. Nevertheless, most of the pieces were retrieved and the stele is now in the Louvre Museum in Paris, France.

**◄ The stele erected by King Mesha of Moab to celebrate his victories.**

## Ahab's house of ivory

There is one Bible story concerning Omri's son, Ahab, that was unexpectedly proved right. It was said that Ahab built a house of ivory at Samaria which seemed unlikely, but when the site was excavated in the 1930s, large numbers of carved ivory plaques were found. It was then clear that certainly the furniture and perhaps even the walls in Ahab's palace were decorated with ivory. These beautiful pieces were largely made by Phoenician craftspeople whose influence in the area was increased by Ahab's marriage to a Phoenician princess, Jezebel. Ahab was killed by his own general, Jehu, who then made himself king.

▲ **A Phoenician ivory carving, from the eighth century BC found at Nimrud, Iraq.**

▲ **Part of the Black Obelisk showing King Jehu of Israel bowing down to the Assyrian king, Shalmaneser III.**

## The Assyrians

It was probably the great wealth of Israel and Judah that attracted the Assyrians to the area. The famous Black Obelisk was found in the Assyrian city of Nimrud by a British archaeologist, Sir Austen Henry Layard, in the 1840s. It shows Jehu as one of the defeated kings bowing down before the Assyrian king, Shalmaneser III. Many Phoenician ivories have been found at the Assyrian capital Nineveh – they may have been looted from ancient Israel. The Assyrians finally invaded both kingdoms, destroying many cities and making Israel into part of their empire. Judah was also defeated and rebellions there were crushed.

▲ **This relief shows an Assyrian army, led by King Sennacherib, scaling the walls of Lachish in 701 BC.**

Like the Egyptians the Assyrians recorded their exploits in great carved reliefs. One of them, now in the British Museum, in London, shows their capture of Lachish in 701 BC. Excavations there have revealed the Assyrian siege ramp and the subsequent destruction of the city. However, there was some settlement by the Assyrians and in another reinterpretation of the early excavations at Gezer it was found that there had been an Assyrian palace there too.

## The Babylonians

The Assyrian empire was eventually taken over by the Babylonians in 612 BC. The Babylonians also swept through Judah and Israel, attacking cities, such as Lachish, which shows signs of destruction from this time.

Finally in 586 BC the Babylonians destroyed Jerusalem, including the great Temple of Solomon. The Hebrew people were taken captive and brought to Babylon. It was during this 47-year exile that many of the books of the Old Testament were finally written down by the Hebrews. When the Babylonian empire was taken over by the Persians in 539 BC the Hebrews returned to their homelands. Amongst the exiles was Nehemiah, whom the Persians made a governor of the province which they also called Judah. His reports on its condition at the time are contained in the Old Testament's *Book of Nehemiah*. There are also traces of Persian occupation in Palestine at Lachish and Beth Shan.

# Alexander and his successors

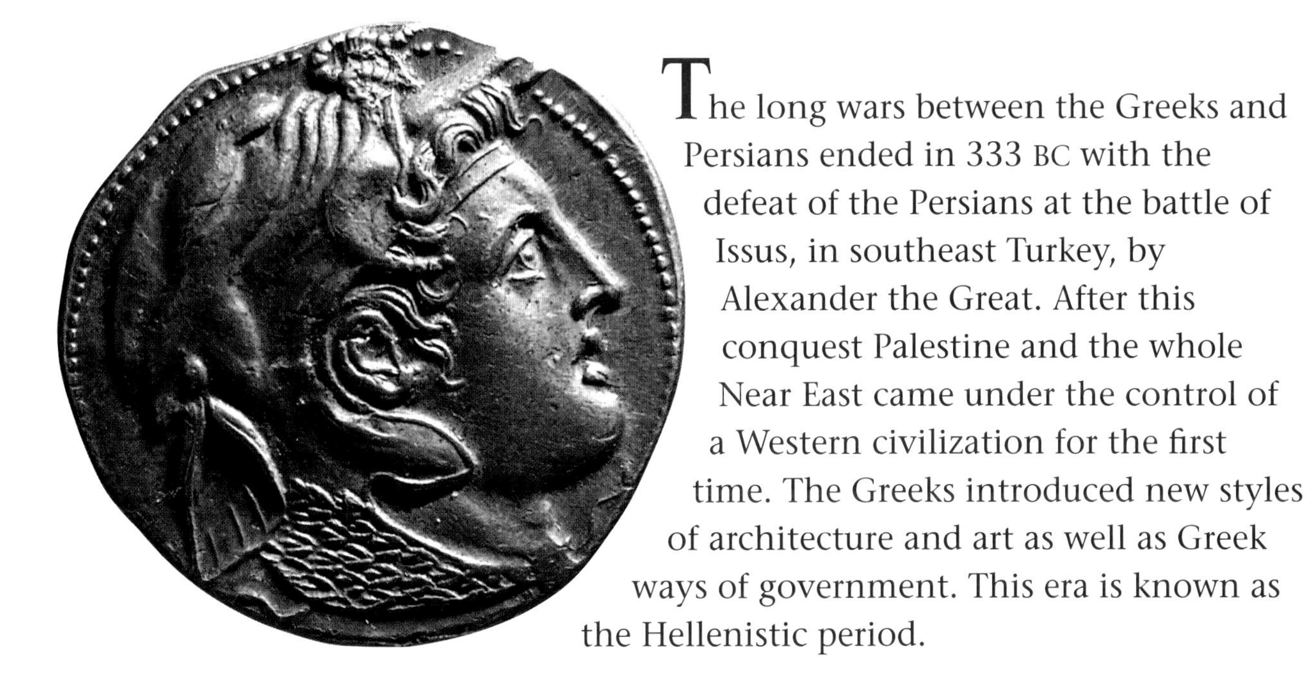

The long wars between the Greeks and Persians ended in 333 BC with the defeat of the Persians at the battle of Issus, in southeast Turkey, by Alexander the Great. After this conquest Palestine and the whole Near East came under the control of a Western civilization for the first time. The Greeks introduced new styles of architecture and art as well as Greek ways of government. This era is known as the Hellenistic period.

**▲ The famous general and ruler Alexander the Great, shown on a silver coin from the Phoenician city of Tyre.**

## Greek rule

After the death of Alexander in Babylon, in 323 BC, his enormous empire was carved up between his squabbling generals. The two most successful were Ptolemy, who founded his own new Egyptian kingdom, and Seleucos, who made himself king of Syria. Palestine was fought over by the two and was under Ptolemaic (Greek-Egyptian) control until 198 BC when it became part of the Seleucid (Greek-Syrian) empire. About thirty years later there was a revolt in Palestine against these Greek rulers, led by a native Jewish dynasty (family) called the Maccabees. The Maccabaean kingdom kept its independence until 63 BC when the whole area, including what was left of the Seleucid empire in Syria, fell to the Roman general Pompey.

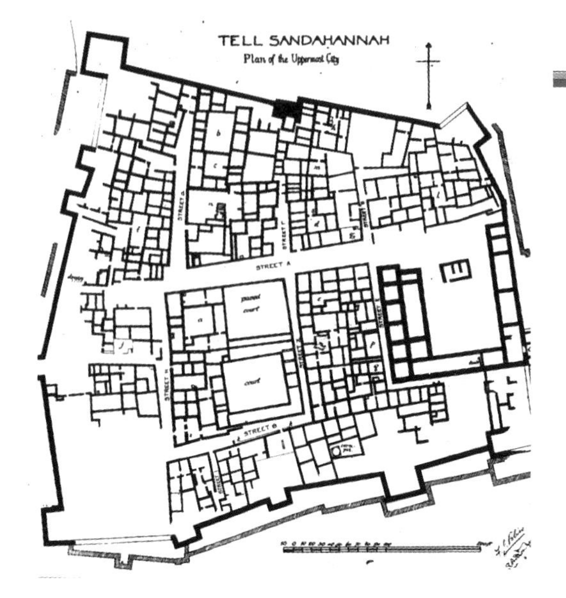


▲ **Bliss and Macalister's plan of Tell Sandahannah, the Hellenistic city of Marissa.**

## Marissa – Bliss and Macalister find a Hellenistic city

In the early Hellenistic period many of the older tells continued to be occupied but were rebuilt in the Greek style of architecture. The most complete view of such a site comes from one of the oldest excavations in the country. In 1900, Frederick Bliss and Robert Macalister excavated Tell Sandahannah, which was identified with the Biblical city of Mareshah (renamed Marissa by the Greeks). In just a few months the archaeologists stripped the entire top surface of the tell to reveal the complete Hellenistic walled city – showing the street layout, private houses and even two buildings which may have been temples or government blocks. To preserve this Hellenistic level no excavations to deeper layers from earlier periods have been made.

## Roman influence on building

When the Romans controlled Palestine, from 63 BC to AD 324, their new cities were usually built on the flat land at the base of the mounds of old tells. The Roman cities show a new architectural style and highlight the influence of the Roman empire on daily life, such as buildings for new cultural activities, especially theatres, and aqueducts to supply water. Recent excavations at Beth Shan are revealing much of the Roman city. Here, there are great wide streets lined with temples, theatres, shops and houses. There is also a wealth of inscriptions, statues and coins that tell us much about daily life in Roman society in Palestine.

◄ **The ruins of the Roman city of Scythopolis with the ancient tell of Beth Shan in the background.**

# Herod, Jesus and the early Church

In 63 BC the Roman general Pompey the Great brought Palestine within the Roman Empire. At first the area was administered from the new province of Syria but in 30 BC a kingdom of Judaea, the Greek name for Judah, was created. The Romans chose as king a man who became one of the ablest and most ruthless of politicians – Herod the Great. Other parts of the country were administered directly by the Romans through governors, known as procurators.

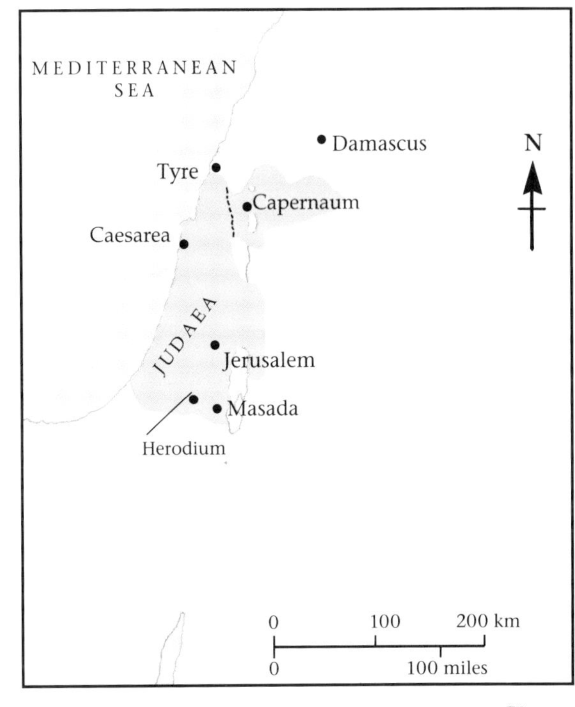


▲ **The coloured area shows the region controlled by Rome. Judaea was governed by Herod the Great.**

## Caesarea and other Herodian constructions

Herod organized great building projects and he introduced many Roman forms of architecture into Palestine. One of his greatest creations was the rebuilding of an old settlement on the coast as the new city of Caesarea, which remained important throughout the Roman period.

◄ **This aerial photograph of Caesarea shows Herod's theatre (centre), built in Hellenistic style, which was changed to a Roman style many years later.**

In 1961 an inscription in honour of the emperor Tiberius was found which had been commissioned by the Roman procurator Pontius Pilatus – who is mentioned in the New Testament.

▲ This aqueduct was built by Herod to bring fresh water into his new coastal city at Caesarea.

Herod was also responsible for new buildings at Samaria and other cities, as well as for a number of forts and private palaces, such as Masada on a mountain near the Dead Sea. He largely rebuilt Jerusalem with new walls, streets and monuments. He also created a magnificent new temple to replace King Solomon's Temple which had been destroyed by the Babylonians.

▲ A model of Herod's Temple.

This model reconstruction of the Herodian Jerusalem is on display at the Hilton Hotel, Jerusalem. ►

## Jesus' time

Unlike the Old Testament, the story of the New Testament mainly concerns individual people and the places where they lived or visited. Whereas great battles or invasions leave tell-tale physical remains for archaeologists to pinpoint, these events did not. We can be fairly sure that Herod's Jerusalem was the city that Jesus knew. Most of the places recorded in the Gospels are well known from earlier periods and as Roman sites, so we know these places existed at that time.

**▲ Remains of a first-century AD house at Capernaum, thought to be where Jesus is believed to have cured St Peter's mother.**

However an episode in the early life of Jesus has been brought to light by archaeological excavations at Capernaum, on the shore of the Sea of Galilee. A synagogue was revealed to have been built over a first-century AD synagogue, which may have been the one Jesus knew. Elsewhere in the town excavations on the site of a Byzantine church revealed that it had been built around a crude house of the first century AD, which had a central room with plastered walls.

Of course, there can be no positive proof but the room has usually been identified as the house of St Peter and the place where Jesus is believed to have healed Peter's mother.

# Revolt against Roman rule

The period covered by the New Testament lasts until the death of St Paul in Rome, in about AD 60, although the Gospel accounts are thought to have been written down a little later. This chapter may also be called 'After the Bible'.

At the time that the Christian Church was growing there was much Jewish discontent in Palestine, due to increased taxes and a hatred of Roman rule. A great revolt of the Jews broke out in AD 66 and a large Roman force was sent to the area in order to control it. The battles raged for four years until Jerusalem was finally captured by Titus, the son of the emperor Vespasian. The city and Herod's Temple were destroyed. Today only the western wall of the Temple platform survives and it is regarded as sacred by Jews as a reminder of their lost temple.

**▲ King Herod's mountain-top palace at the northern end of Masada. On the top are the remains of storerooms and the defensive wall around the edge. During the siege the Romans built a huge earth ramp up to the wall, so that they could break through it and capture the palace, in AD 73.**

## The siege of Masada

The final battle of the revolt against Rome was at Masada. This was where Herod had built himself a luxurious palace in the hills near the Dead Sea, but by 70 AD it was occupied by the last Jewish rebels and was besieged by the Romans. The history of this siege is preserved in the writings of the Jewish historian Josephus, who records how the defenders finally committed mass suicide rather than be captured by the Romans. Excavations here led by Yigael Yadin in 1963–5 revealed the accuracy of Josephus' description of the tragic end. Scattered over the palace were the remains of hundreds of skeletons, and even pieces of pottery with numbers painted on them, which the defenders drew to decide who should kill the others.

**Painted pottery pieces found at Masada. ►**

▲ **One of the Dead Sea Scrolls. The age of these scrolls is disputed but most people now believe they go back to the second century BC.**

## Qumran and the Dead Sea Scrolls

Not far from Masada lie the ruins of a small settlement called Qumran. This was founded in the second century BC by a sect of Jews called the Essenes. During the period of the revolt, in AD 66, when there was danger all around, many of the Essenes fled into nearby caves taking their sacred writings with them. In 1948 a shepherd boy, wandering into one of the caves, found ancient scrolls in pottery storage jars. These, the famous Dead Sea Scrolls, contained some of the earliest surviving fragments of the Old Testament written in Hebrew. Excavations at the site of Qumran have revealed what was probably the room where the scrolls were written along with more of the storage jars.

▲ **The ruins of Qumran with the mountains behind, where many of the Dead Sea Scrolls were found.**

## Mosaic map of Palestine

Roman rule in the second and third centuries AD was a period of prosperity and many monuments date from this period. After the Roman Empire was converted to Christianity in the early fourth century AD it became

known as the Byzantine Empire. In this period many churches were built on ancient sites of Christian interest. The floors of these churches were often covered with beautiful mosaics – one of the most famous is at Madeba, in Jordan, which forms a great map of Palestine and the surrounding lands. Byzantine Palestine was invaded by Arabs, in the early seventh century AD, who were spreading the new religion of Islam. Their Dome of the Rock mosque in Jerusalem is one of the earliest and the most beautiful in the area and it is believed to have been built over the site of Herod's Temple. Tradition also relates the site to the Patriarch, Abraham, and the Islamic prophet Muhammad, and it is thus an area held sacred by Jews, Christians and Muslims alike.

## 'Cradle of Civilization'

Over the last 150 years archaeologists have excavated hundreds of Biblical sites in Palestine and the surrounding area, covering thousands of years of history. This area has been called the 'Cradle of Civilization' – for these sites have revealed the introduction of agriculture, metalworking and the manufacture of fine pottery and other beautiful objects. The sites have shown us evidence of the rise and fall of great cities and the passage of succeeding civilizations. There remain many more sites to be discovered and excavated and with the development of archaeology our knowledge of the area is growing all the time. The Bible remains unique as a document and is an invaluable guide to ancient civilizations, but it is only modern archaeology that provides details of these civilizations.

**Part of the mosaic map at Madeba, dated to the sixth century AD.** ▼

# Timeline

| NEOLITHIC 8300–4500 BC | LATE BRONZE AGE 1550–1150 BC |
|---|---|
| Settlement at 'Ain Ghazal.<br>**7000** BC Jericho the first walled town. | Palestine becomes Egyptian province.<br>**1468** BC Tuthmosis III defeats a Canaanite army at Megiddo.<br>Ramesses II builds Pi-Ramesses using Hebrew captives.<br>**c.1200** BC Sea Peoples – including the Philistines – attack Syria, Egypt and Palestine.<br>**c.1150** BC Egypt gives up control of Palestine.<br>Hapiru/Hebrew peoples in Palestine.<br>'Exodus' from Egypt.<br>Joshua – battles of Jericho and Ai. |

| CHALCOLITHIC 4500–3200 BC |
|---|
| Timna copper mines in Negev Desert<br>Ghassoul wall-paintings. |

| EARLY BRONZE AGE 3200–2000 BC | IRON AGE 1200–612 BC |
|---|---|
| Canaanite civilization, trade and cities flourish.<br>Settlement at Ai.<br>Abraham thought to have lived at the city of Ur, Mesopotamia.<br>**c.2400** BC Cities of the Plain destroyed.<br>Contact between Egypt and Palestine. | **Thirteenth to twelfth centuries** BC<br>Rise of 'Israelites'.<br>**1150** BC Philistine settlement in Palestine.<br>**1100** BC Decline of Canaanites.<br>Phoenician civilization.<br>**11th century** Saul ruled. War between Israelites and Philistines.<br>**1000–960** BC David ruled.<br>**930** BC Solomon dies. Split of Judah/Israel.<br>Assyrian invasion of Israel and Judah. |

| MIDDLE BRONZE AGE 2000–1550 BC |
|---|
| **c.1900** BC Egyptian wall-paintings show Canaanite traders.<br>**c.1700** BC Egyptian Middle Kingdom collapses.<br>Hyksos rule in lower Egypt,<br>Joseph possibly lived at this time.<br>**1550** BC Revolt against Hyksos and Egyptians invade Palestine. |

▼ A model of Herod's Temple.

This timeline lists many of the sites and events mentioned in this book.

## BABYLONIAN/PERSIAN
### 612–332 BC

**612** BC Babylonians sweep through Judah and Israel
**586** BC Jerusalem falls
Hebrew people exiled in Babylon for 47 years
**539** BC Persian empire overthrows Babylonian empire

## HELLENISTIC
### 332–63 BC

**332** BC Alexander the Great conquers Persians and takes over Palestine.
**323** BC Alexander dies. Ptolemy controls Egypt (and Palestine) and Seleucos controls Syria.
**198** BC Palestine becomes part of Greek–Syrian Empire.
**c.168** BC Revolt by Maccabaean Kingdom lasts until **63** BC.

## ROMAN/HERODIAN
### 63 BC–AD 324

**63** BC Roman general Pompey controls Syrian empire and Palestine.
**63** BC–AD **324** Roman control of Palestine.
**30** BC Rome created the kingdom of Judaea ruled by Herod the Great.
Period of Jesus' life.
AD **66–73** Jewish Revolt against Rome and siege of Masada.

## BYZANTINE
### AD 324–640

Church of the Holy Sepulchre built where Empress Helena found remains of the 'cross'

## MODERN

**1830s** Edward Robinson explores Bible lands.
**1840s** Sir Austen Layard finds Black Obelisk.
**1867** Captain Charles Warren excavates at Jerusalem.
**1868** Moabite stele found at Dhiban (Dibon).
**1884** Amarna Letters discovered.
**1890** William Flinders Petrie excavates at Tell el-Hesi.
**1899–1900** Frederick Bliss and Robert Macalister excavate at Marissa.
**1902–9** Macalister excavates Gezer – finds Solomonic gateway and 'Hellenistic' fort.
**1930** John Garstang excavates at Jericho.
**1932** Flinders Petrie excavates Tell el-'Ajjul.
**1948** Dead Sea Scrolls found near Qumran.
**1952–8** Dame Kathleen Kenyon works at Jericho.
**1960s** Joseph Callaway excavates at Ai.
**1963–5** Yigael Yadin discovers evidence of siege at Masada.
**1961** Copper objects found at Nahal Mishmar.
**1966** Manfred Bietak excavates Tell el Dab'a.
**1982** Excavations at 'Ain Ghazal.
**1993** 'House of David' stone inscription found at Tel Dan.

# Glossary

**Ammonite** The tribe which lived east of the River Jordan and were enemies of the Israelites.
**Aqueduct** A structure that carries water.
**Archaeologist** A person who studies remains found in the earth to learn more about the past.
**Assyrian** The ancient kingdom of north Mesopotamia which grew into a great empire during 721 and 633 BC.
**Babylonian** The great empire based from the southern kingdom of Mesopotamia, which was at its most powerful between 2200–586 BC.
**Bible** The sacred writings of the Christian religion. It contains accounts of Jesus' life and teachings in the New Testament, and the earlier writings from the Hebrew faith in the Old Testament.
**Byzantine** The Roman Empire in the East after the empire in the West fell in AD 476. The Byzantine Empire lasted from AD 324 to 1453.
**Canaan** An ancient region between the River Jordan and the Mediterranean Sea, where the Canaanite civilization developed in the Early Bronze Age. Regarded as the 'Promised Land' of the Israelites.
**Christianity** The Christian religion, which follows the teachings of Jesus Christ.
**Chronology** A list of times, dates or events arranged in order.
**Crucified** Put to death by an ancient form of execution where the victim was tied or nailed to a cross and left to die.
**Debris** The remains of something which has been broken or destroyed.
**Egyptian Middle Kingdom** The period when Egypt was a powerful state and controlled a huge empire (2040–1782 BC).
**Excavations** The digging work carried out to uncover remains from the past.
**Exile** To be forced to live away from your homeland.
**Fertile** When land can produce many crops.
**Fortifications** Structures which help to defend a place.
**Garrisons** Fortified places which are guarded by soldiers.
**Geometric** Relating to design made up of simple shapes, such as circles and triangles.
**Gospels** The first four books of the New Testament.
**Hittites** The empire from southern Anatolia (modern Turkey), which also controlled Northern Syria around 2000 BC.
**Holy Land** Another name for Palestine.
**Idol** An object which is worshipped as a god.
**Inscriptions** Carved writings, usually in stone.
**Israelites** The ancient peoples who believed they were descended from Jacob. In the Bible, people from the kingdom of Israel (922–721 BC).
**Judaism** The Jewish religion based on the Old Testament and other Hebrew writings.
**Mass suicide** When a group of people take their own lives as a single act, usually as a protest.
**Mosques** Muslim places of worship.
**Muslims** People who follow the religion of Islam.
**Near East** The countries of the eastern Mediterranean.
**Nile Delta** The area at the mouth of the River Nile where it enters the Mediterranean Sea.
**Papyrus** The paper-like material used for writing, made from the grass-like papyrus plant.
**Pilgrims** People who travel to sacred places connected with their religion.
**Province** An area or territory which is ruled by another country.
**Reliefs** Carved scenes, usually in stone.
**Scarab seals** Egyptian seals in the form of a beetle.
**Sect** A subdivision, or smaller group, of a larger religious group.
**Stele** An upright stone slab decorated with figures or inscriptions.

# Books to read

**Younger Readers**

*Great Events of Bible Times* by Malcolm Day (Marshall Editions Development Ltd., 1994)

**The following have major references to lands and civilizations mentioned in this book:**

*The Ancient World* (Historical Atlas series) by John Briquebec (Kingfisher Books, 1990)

*Early Civilizations* (The Usborne Illustrated World History) by Jane Chisholm and Anne Millard (Usborne Publishing Ltd., 1991)

*First Civilizations* (Cultural Atlas for Young People) by Erica C. D. Hunter, PH.D. (Facts on File/Andromeda Oxford Ltd., 1994)

**Older readers**

*Archaeological Encyclopaedia of the Holy Land* ed. by Negev (Prentice-Hall, 1991)

*Archaeology* (Eyewitness Guides) by Jane McIntosh (Dorling Kindersley, 1994)

*Bible Lands* (Eyewitness Guides) by Jonathan Tubb (Dorling Kindersley, 1991)

*Great Events of Bible Times* ed. by James Harpur (Weidenfield and Nicholson, 1987)

# Museums to visit or contact

**Britain**

Ashmolean Museum
Beaumont Street
Oxford, OX1 2PH
Tel: (01865) 512651

The British Museum
Great Russell Street
London
WC1B 3DG
Tel: (0171) 636 1555

Edinburgh University,
Department of Archaeology
Teaching Collection
16–20 George Square
Edinburgh
EH8 9JZ
Tel: (0131) 667 1011

Fitzwilliam Museum
Trumpington Street
Cambridge
CB2 1RB
Tel: (01223) 337733/332900

**Eire**

Chester Beatty Library and
Gallery of Oriental Art
20 Shrewsbury Road, Dublin 4
Tel: (00) (353) (01)
692386/695187

Weingreen Museum of Biblical
Antiquities
Trinity College
Dublin 2
Tel: (00) (353) (01) 772491

**France**

The Louvre Museum
Cour Napoleon
Paris, 75001
Tel: (00) (33) (1) 40205050

# Index

Entries in **bold** indicate illustrations.